# EYES OF THE DRAGON:
# IN HONOR OF KIM JONG UN

By

**Geoffrey A. Todd**

ISBN: 9781096503316

# DEDICATION

In honor of the Chairman of the Workers' Party of Korea and the Supreme Commander of the Korean People's Army, who has many other titles, Kim Jong Un, on the occasion of the birthday of his father, Eternal General Secretary and Leader, Kim Jong Il, February 16th, Juche 107 (2018).

G. A. Todd

# AUTHOR'S NOTE

The author was very pleased to receive the request to write this book.  Please be aware that the author is not attempting to teach *Juche* Ideology to those who know it far better than himself, but is striving to show how that Ideology supports resistance to sanctions.  Hopefully the non-Korean reader will come away from this book with a new appreciation for the futility and cruelty of sanctions and the ridiculous nature of the demand for the DPRK to give up their nuclear weapons.  Any mistakes are entirely the fault of the author and not of those who requested the production of this work.

G. A. Todd

# CONTENTS

# CHAPTER ONE: *INVOCATION OF THE HEROES*.

1    Kim Jong Un smiled—it was an auspicious day,

And he had helped make it better still,

By uniting, in a glorious way,

All Korea, under his generous will.


5    He had granted the world, through diplomacy shrewd,

The vision of Korea that he had in mind,

A vision of unity, where no enemy would intrude,

A vision of glory Kim Jong Un's father would find

Well-nurtured by the son that he left behind,

10    Who cared for the people they had imbued

With grandeur and magnificence and banners

    entwined

At the Olympics, on his birthday, all Korea

    renewed.


For it was the Sixteenth of February,

A Holy Day, as the world now could see,

15    And Kim Jong Un, ever insightful and ready,

Had honored Leader Kim Jong Il's destiny.


For from ages past ancient past Time past forever

Kim Jong Il had been destined to take the command

From the Mighty Kim Il Sung and then hand their

    endeavor

20    To Kim Jong Un, today's Leader of Korea, Holy Land.

Kim Jong Un smiled, but he knew his work was not

    done,

He knew he had to remain alert every second,

For without his attention peace could not be won,

And Eternal Korea his genius now beckoned.


25    But as the Democratic People's Republic of Korea

Now shone in pageantry on the world's bright

    stage,

The Supreme Commander looked back in Time to see a

History that his Great Leader Father had waged.


As the banners waved in colors so bright,

30    And the dancers danced to music triumphant,

Kim thought of his father, who in his might,

Had made the plans of other world leaders

redundant.


Not just military might, but mental might too—

Kim Jong Il held every nation in check

35    As he worked to develop what was then brand new:

Nuclear weapons to free the DPRK's neck

From the yoke other nations would try to impose

To steal from Korea her resources and freedom,

And to keep her citizens enthralled in the throes

40    Of tame insignificance and powerless fiefdom.


And Kim Jong Un in his own brilliance

These wise policies advanced,

And made his country even more resilient,

As he made sure its fate was not left to chance.


45    For now Korea's nuclear power was so great,

That every nation listened if Kim even whispered;

Korea thus controlled its own fate,

And under such identity had prospered.


Kim Jong Un's eyes narrowed—as sharp as an eagle—

50    His aspect was now one of anger and fury,

There was no one on earth more dreadful and regal,

And any person seeing him would bow in a hurry.


For in spite of what his father had done,

In spite of all that he himself had continued,

55    The world was acting as if a peace could be won

By depriving the DPRK of its nuclear sinew

And leaving it powerless against every blow

Enemy or invader would happily dish out,

As if Korea was somehow too stupid to know

60    That such a destruction was sure to come about.


There was one way to peace, and Kim knew it well,

The world had to accept his country's power,

And not doubt for an instant he could unleash hell,

If someone wished to impose slavery's dark hour.


65    Kim Jong Un, Wisest of Leaders

Was resisting, not asking, for war,

Anyone except enemy deceivers.

Could see peace was what he hoped for.

Yet now the UN was making sanctions

70      That threatened the peace which Kim sought,

For they were hurting the nation

Which the deaths of heroes had bought.


Millions had died for this country,

And Kim had seen all of their names,

75      Who was obscure and forgotten by many,

Kim knew and leant them his fame.


For now he embodied the fallen,

And he now the living had to preserve,

And no citizen of his would be called when

80      Some other country demanded they serve.

Great Kim! The people need you now

More than ever to maintain control,

For the country that to an invader must bow,

Loses not just its borders, but its soul!

# CHAPTER TWO: *MORE THAN A GENERALISSIMO.*

85     Kim was sitting in his box on a balcony

      Above a crowded auditorium and stage,

      He also had a sophisticated screen he could see,

      To make sure the Olympics were fairly waged.


      Kim intimately understood every sport,

90     And could of course have pursued any one,

      But he had activities of greater import

      That he had to make sure were well done.


      For he oversaw all military training,

      Including Korea's elite Special Forces,

95    And he taught them by action, not just by explaining,

Even showing them how to ride horses.


Kim had scoured the world for the best

Of Martial Arts for his men to apply,

He personally had given each system a test

100   To make sure his soldiers got by.


And not just got by, but powerfully won,

So powerfully they held every country in awe,

For, make no mistake, Kim had tried every one,

Even Brazilian Ju-Jitsu and Krav Maga.


105   So Kim had developed a secret fighting system,

Much of which was only known by his secret corps,

And though highly-qualified, Kim still would assist them,

And teach their trainers the art of hand-to-hand war.


And broader strategy Kim also mastered,

110   Sun-Tzu, Von Clausewitz, and the rest—

Kim Il Sung and Kim Jong Il wrote wisest, thought faster,

So that Kim Jong Un himself became best.


But Nuclear Warfare was Kim's specialty—

How far removed from Figure Skating was this!

115   Nuclear Realpolitik shaped Kim's identity—

At least to those who feared Kim's Nuclear Fist.


Kim was the master of Nuclear Logic,

While other nations acted like blindfolded fools,

With a single question he made them seem tragic,

*120*    And took their ambassadors to school.


For example, when asked to unilaterally surrender

His Nuclear Arsenal by representatives from the West,

He said simply, "I don't seem to remember

The U.S. doing this when Russia thought it best."


*125*    But Kim's people knew him as more than just wise,

More than a genius or Generalissimo,

For the fortunate ones who looked into Kim's eyes

Saw a Person of Eternal Soul.


So it was suddenly when in rushed a child,

*130*    A little girl barely older than five;

Kim's Adjutant-General was none to mild,

When he grabbed her to push her outside.


"Wait!" said Kim, "Let the girl go,

It's obvious she has something important to say.

135    Now child," he said, "do let me know

Why it is you have come here on this Holy Day."

# CHAPTER THREE: *THE DREAM OF THE LITTLE GIRL.*

"Dear Leader, Father," the little girl began,

"I was sent here by a confusing dream.

I don't dream often, although I can,

140    But this one was different, or so it seemed."


"What do you mean 'sent'?" Kim Jong Un asked.

"I mean I was sent by one everybody knows well:

Dear Leader Kim Jong Il gave me this task."

"I see, child, you do have a story to tell."


145    "Thank you, Daddy," the little girl said,

Forgetting about formal protocol:

The Adjutant-General nearly came out of his head;

"It's okay," said Kim, "I don't mind it at all."


The girl crawled onto the Father-Leader's knee—

150    Here was a child innocent and pure!

Like a Colossus Kim strode the world scene,

But with this Gentle Giant the girl felt secure.


She began her story after a pause,

For a moment very deep in thought.

155    "I fell asleep easily, I don't know the dream's cause,

But it must by Leader Kim Jong Il have been brought.


"In the dream I was walking in a flowery meadow,

Birds were chirping and butterflies landed nearby,

Things were as peaceful as things can go,

160   When suddenly a tiny mouse caught my eye.


"For some reason, just being in a dream I guess,

I could understand what the mouse was saying,

He was very agitated—shaking, no less—

And said 'We must seek shelter without delaying.'


165   "I tried to ask him why, but he just said 'Please hurry!'

And so I followed wherever he ran,

All over the sizable meadow he scurried,

As if without direction or plan.


"This went on for a very long while,

170   Jumping that way and this way and this;

I was almost worn out," she said with a smile,

"But it was a dream so to scurry I could not resist.


"Then suddenly, streaking down from the sky

Falcon after falcon dove for the mouse,

175    But they couldn't quite reach him—he somehow got

       by—

As if protected by an invisible house.


"All this time I was getting more worried

What if the falcons came after me?

The faster and faster we hurried,

180    My terror grew and would not let me be.


"Then with horror I saw them up in the sky,

The falcons, like vultures, had grouped all together,

And it seemed that at me they were aiming to fly.

I watched them prepare, and it seemed like forever

185    When, whoosh!—Gentle hands lifted the mouse high,

And I fell at the feet of a very strong man,

I looked up and saw into the Dear Leader's eyes

And felt peace as peaceful as any peace can.


"But Daddy, it wasn't over—it wasn't over quite yet,

190    For the circling birds began a swift dive,

And you should have seen it, in spite of the threat,

Leader Kim Jong Il knew we would survive;

For he held the mouse in one hand and then

With the other swatted the birds to the side:

195    Where a normal man hits one, the Dear Leader hit ten,

And the birds their meal of a girl were denied.

"Then he told me, 'Young lady, what you have seen

Remember, for it is my gift to you.

Now go to the Great Father and say where you've

    been—

200   He'll tell you what it means and what to do.'


"So Daddy, I've come here, just like I was told,

Though my parents were against it out of respect,

But because of the Dear Leader I was made bold,

And snuck here so I wouldn't his orders neglect."


205   "You did the right thing, child," the Dear Father said,

"And I'll tell your parents that all is well.

The dream is important that was placed in your head,

The Dear Leader had a crucial story to tell.

"For you need not be afraid any more,

210    I am here like my Father who came ahead of me,

And, as you know, he is here like before,

To guide you with something you can see.


"The mouse, little child, represents your fears,

That led you in circles when they were followed;

215    When the falcons attacked it, it didn't disappear,

Because your fears by themselves can't be swallowed.


"For the falcons are the missiles that keep you afraid,

Which you fear the enemy will send any night,

Which is why by your fears you are always waylaid,

220    When enemy schemes keep you quaking in fright.

"But child, my Father was there you to save,

And he sent you to me on this Holy Day

So I could assure you to remain brave;

For, like the Dear Leader, I will get in the way

225 Of any missile launch the enemy would plan;

For my family is here to protect you, young rose,

And, as you saw, we have strength in our hands,

And only a fool would us with weapons oppose."


With that the girl smiled and on her way went,

230 Comforted by her Father's words and his Soul,

Very glad the Dear Leader herself to him had sent,

And trusting in his strong hands of control.

Kim looked after her with a strengthened resolve—

He had to find peace to avoid any loss;

235    But it was a difficult problem to solve,

For he could not sanction peace at a reckless cost.


Then suddenly came struggling in through the door,

An eight-year-old boy, "Let me in!" he shouted,

Kim told the Adjutant, "If we get any more,

240    Let them in also, my Father must not be doubted."


"Reporting for duty, Supreme Commander!"

The boy crisply saluted with pride and with spirit,

"A vicious snow-leopard has got up my dander,

And the Dear Leader himself wants you to hear it."

# CHAPTER FOUR: *THE DREAM OF THE YOUNG BOY.*

245     "At ease, young soldier," the Great Leader said.

"Have a seat and tell me all you have dreamt,

For it would be rotten if I didn't listen instead,

For I would be holding my Father in contempt."


"Supreme Commander, I was dreaming most gently,

250     Walking by a forest on a mountainside trail,

When I began to listen most intently,

As fear came down on me like a sinister veil.


"I began to walk more nervously and quickly;

I moved even faster, feeling more dread.

255    I'm young and strong and not at all sickly,

But I was growing weaker and weaker instead.

"It wasn't just weakness, but also great hunger,

And then I heard a loud snarl and a growl;

Though losing strength I knew I couldn't linger,

260    And my stomach began to feel very foul.

"I ran and ran as rapidly as ever,

And chanced a swift glance over one shoulder—

I was being pursued by a great snow leopard,

Who was leaping from boulder to boulder!

265    "Surprisingly, it spoke, taking a moment to laugh,

'You think you're hungry—what about me?

But I'll have a full stomach once you've felt my wrath,

And from your hunger pangs you'll also be free.'


"Funny thing though, it seemed it spoke English,

270    Which somehow I seemed to understand;

I don't know if American, Australian, or British,

I just know it was strange to hear in our land.


"I veered quickly into the nearby woods,

Growing more feeble as I rushed past the trees;

275    Now it seemed if I tried I almost could

Feel the beast's hot breath: I grew weak in the knees.


"'I've got you now!' the beast hungrily said,

And I felt his long tongue tasting my back.

I knew then for certain I soon would be dead,

280    So I swung around like a man to face the attack.


"But before he leapt to tear me to pieces,

Before even his claws tore my skin,

Suddenly from his hunger I felt great release as

A strong and brave man between us jumped in.


285    "With his mighty hand he grabbed the beast's neck,

Then reached in with the other and tore out its tongue,

The beast let out a scream as the man threw that wreck

Past the tops of the trees just beneath the bright sun.


"Then I looked, and I saw—the Dear Leader's eyes!

290    It was he who had saved me, he who was strong!

He smiled and my hunger seemed like only lies

That vanish whenever the Truth comes along.


"I felt renewed strength, and he started to speak

In a voice as gentle as a deep-flowing stream;

295    I soared as though lifted to a high mountain peak,

In this greatest of wonderful dreams.


"'Be brave, my good boy,' he said with a smile,

'For the Great Leader is working even now

To fight the sanctions, so cruel a trial,

300    Through which other countries would force us to bow.


"'Go to the Supreme Commander, he'll

Hear you out, once you tell him you come from me;

Then he'll give you orders and specifically tell

Exactly the kind of soldier you should be.'


305   "With that I woke up, feeling very good,

And I knew what precisely I should do:

I came here as fast as I possibly could,

To immediately request direct orders from you."


The Supreme Commander smiled, for here was a boy

310   Who was keen both to learn and obey.

"You have done well, young soldier, for I get no joy

When the leopards of hunger on our people prey.


"We must fight these cruel sanctions together:

Supreme Commander, farmer, soldier, woman, man;

315 We need children like you to help our endeavor

By encouraging the young ones to make a brave stand.


"It's obvious the enemy means to starve us—

They care not for the innocent girl or boy;

They work toward the destruction of our harvest,

320 And to the obliteration of all of life's joys.


"They block food to force us into submission,

Telling us to do an illogical thing:

They have put us in a nearly impossible position

Of starvation or missile surrendering.


325 "But we will fight with our blockade runners,

With citizen-smugglers and business-warriors too,

We'll attack them with computer-commando gunners,

And show what determined minds can do.


"Spread the word, boy—the people are resisting!

330    Together we'll win, but in disunity fail;

In training and hope keep persisting,

And follow me to the peak at the end of the trail!"


"Yes, Supreme Commander!" the boy bravely said,

As he leapt to his feet and sharply saluted.

335    Watching him leave Kim's thoughts turned deep red

Against those whose logic was so easily refuted

And who still would try to starve innocent children

As though his people were pawns without hearts,

As though loving parents wouldn't by grief be killed

    when

340   The enemy's tactics tore their babies apart.


Was this the noble Geneva Convention?

Liberty and Happiness' lawful pursuit?

Was this somehow Love's sacred intervention,

Or did the enemy their own hearts confute?


345   Suddenly the Great Leader heard glorious music,

And put earbuds in from his large screen,

The People's Symphony was at the Olympics,

And to hear their perfection Kim was keen.

# CHAPTER FIVE: *MUSIC OF THE DEFIANT.*

Kim listened with pleasure at the glorious stanzas,

350    The precise percussion and smooth violins,

The amazing talent perfection demands as

The artistry of emotion was woven in.


Kim knew the notes intimately—how could he not?

For he himself was their Great Inspiration;

355    It was the Dear Father who created each thought,

For the Dear Father embodied the Sacred Nation.


The strings flowed beautifully like mountain rivers,

The woodwinds were forests alive in the breeze,

The grandeur of the percussion sent shivers

360    The global audience felt in their knees.

Now the conductor was capturing emotion,

Because the Dear Father was first in his heart;

The music began from a delicate notion

To grow and tear Time's very fabric apart.


365    The strings cascaded in layers like torrents,

The woodwinds felled forests with their might,

The beat of the percussion became such a portent

That only the virtuous were not left in fright.


For now the world once again saw

370    Who they were daring to antagonize:

Like the deep lake after the thaw,

They were getting a glimpse into the Great Leader's

    eyes.

Those eyes of power, those eye of rage,

Eyes that warned all to fear his great wrath;

375     No one must dare war to casually wage,

Or continue down sanctions' reckless path!


The violin bows in those eye became rockets

In artillery batteries aimed at the foe;

The big bass bassoon filled the nuclear docket,

380     And left no doubt where the nuclear missiles would go.


The crescendo of harmony became overwhelming,

As those eyes grew yet deeper still;

The honest listener knew there was no overcoming

The Leader who those sounds could fill.

*385*  Then on the stage came the beautiful maidens—

No greater beauty has the world ever seen!—

Who of their Great Leader with remarkable cadence,

Sang praises with their voices bright and keen.


Their Father's eyes softened to see such good

children,

*390*  To hear the praises they sang from their hearts;

For his gentle eyes told of no greater thrill than

When the girls of Korea such joy would impart.


The Great Leader smiled and his earbuds removed;

He was glad for the talks that he'd started;

*395*  Now perhaps some discord could be soothed,

And some wisdom learned from what he'd imparted.

Then into his private luxury box

Was ushered a middle-aged mother and wife;

"I had a dream, Great Leader, where darkness stalks,

400   But the Dear Leader himself saved my life."

# CHAPTER SIX: *THE DREAM OF THE WIFE AND MOTHER.*

"Dear lady, don't be nervous," said the Great Kim,

For her voice had been shaky and she seemed very

    scared,

"Have a sip of some tea, and let calmness sink in,

Since for your story I'm very well prepared."


405    The woman took a drink and, feeling better,

Composed herself and sank into thought:

Something dramatic had happened to upset her,

And she wanted to be certain that nothing was forgot.


"Great Leader, I was dreaming deeply last night,

410    Compelled into a sleep I had never known,

When suddenly I realized with joy and with fright,

That into an antelope I'd somehow grown.


"It was great, I was youthful, and beautiful too;

I leapt with the herd in great delight;

415    We laughed and cavorted all the day through,

Until an exquisite fawn sprang into my sight.


"I knew instantly somehow that this was my boy,

Joining me mystically within my own dream;

Some great secret power someone had to employ

420    To carry out so momentous a scheme.


"For once again let me say that this dream was different,

Not normal in almost any way,

I was tingling with smells and sights so magnificent

That I knew someone had planned that bouquet.


125     "My son and I, filled with joy, were running and dancing,

And somehow went astray from the galloping herd;

We didn't notice it had happened until stopped in our

    prancing

By something that terror in our hearts greatly stirred.


"It was a low growl, coming from behind us;

130     I knew at once that it was a tiger;

There was no chance that anyone would find us,

Before he tore us fiber from fiber.


"I turned around quickly and the tiger roared;

I kept my nerve for the sake of my fawn:

*435*   'Please, Sir Tiger, I earnestly implored,

Take me and let my son hurry on.'


"'I am the Tiger,' said the great beast,

'You are just another morsel to me;

Why in the world should your fawn be released,

*440*   When a tasty hors d'oeuvre is all that I see?'


"'Lord Tiger,' I said, grasping at straws,

'Surely you want my offspring to live;

He can then breed and by Natural Laws

You'll feed off what Nature then gives.'


*445*   "The tiger laughed loudly, 'I have food everywhere;

I have generations of offspring upon whom to feast.

How is it to insult my intelligence you dare?'

And again roared and then laughed the great beast.


"I was at my wits' end, we were as good as dead,

450    I couldn't think of any argument to advance;

Then suddenly a thought leapt into my head,

And, desperate, I decided to give it a chance.


"'Tiger, Your Majesty,' I said carefully,

'If you will first let my skinny son go,

455    I'll betray a confidence held secretly,

That only fully-grown antelopes know.'


"'You must be crazy,' said the mighty tiger,

'You're hardly in a position to bargain with me.'

"'But Lord,' I said, 'wouldn't it be wiser

460  My bargaining position to truly see?'


"'Okay then, spit it out, but you are testing my patience,

You have just an instant before I swallow you whole.'

'I'll show you the secret pasture, the residence,

Where all of the antelopes feed their weary souls

465  When they need a break from wandering and hiding,

From dodging predators and fighting the snow,

Where they fatten themselves by grasses imbibing—

I'll show you all of this if you'll let my son go.'"


"The tiger thought a moment, and then said with a grin,

470  'I'll let your son go and as you say you will do,

And then when I know how to find all your kin,

I'll eagerly make a meal out of you.'

"'It's a deal,' I agreed, silently planning.

'Let me say a final good-bye to my son.'

475     I turned to the boy, who had no understanding

Of the terrible bargain we'd done.


"'Now son, I want you to run far away,

And when you're weary, then practice hiding;

I'll return sometime tomorrow or today,

480     And quickly discover where you've been abiding.'


"My boy galloped away, and the tiger laughed and said,

'You understand, of course, I will find him;

You've only saved him a day or so from joining the

        dead.'

I said 'Yes, but I hope you'll be too full to dine him.'"

485   "I led the huge tiger at a light run,

His hot breath beside and behind me,

I knew one false move and I'd be undone,

As the tiger was quick to remind me:


"'If you even take an unusual breath,

490   If you skip instead of naturally striding,

Then you will meet an unnatural death,

And I'll hurry to where your son is hiding.'


"The confident tiger had no idea

He had bargained with the wrong mother and wife:

495   Let no one dare challenge the women of Korea!—

The antelope pasture was the afterlife.

"There was no meadow where he could eat his fill—

Don't mess with a mother and her only child!—

I was going to send this bastard straight to hell,

500    And his death would be brutal, not mild!


"I began to gradually run a bit faster,

Somehow knowing where I should turn,

Then suddenly, at a bend, at the risk of disaster,

I sprinted ahead before the Tiger could discern

505    What was my intent, and that I had learned

How to make his own instinct an irrational master

And use his own anger his logic to spurn—

For when sprints an antelope, few beasts can catch her.

"I knew I had but a few seconds at most,

510    But I had the initiative and spirit;

Soon I would have to give up the ghost,

But because of my fawn I didn't fear it.

"One more turn!  There it was! I called back at the tiger,

'Hey stupid! Just try to make a meal out of me!'

515    The monster's eyes narrowed, its mouth opened wider,

And I led him over a steep cliff and was free.

"The tiger screamed horribly, but I leapt with joy:

He leapt into terror, I leapt into life—

For now I knew I had saved my dear boy,

520    Like any good Korean mother and wife.

"I was falling happily to my death—

I was almost down to the rocks below,

When suddenly, as quick as the North Wind's breath,

Someone swooped down fast and low

525    And as rapidly as rapid has ever been,

Faster than any bird of prey,

Swifter than the typhoon rushes in,

A man on a Chollima bore me away!


"The tiger was mangled on the rocks behind us

530    As the man's strong arm held me tight;

The beautiful Chollima in an instant aligned us

With the stars that began to shine in the night.

"I could feel the kindness from the man's heart;

I did not have to look to know his name:

535    Too often in life had I been a part

Of the love and the honor he'd daily proclaimed.


"He was Kim Jong Il, the Beloved Dear Leader,

And into his powerful eyes I gazed;

In *Juche* I was no more profound a believer

540    Than in that moment that seemed to last days.


"Like an eagle we soared, for an eternal instant—

How wonderful was this death after life!

How glorious if this state could be constant

For every Korean mother and wife!

545    "In a breath of forever the Chollima took me

To where my dear fawn was at rest;

There the Dear Leader gently put me

Beside him to sleep the sleep of the blest.


"They were gone like the wind, but their love stayed,

550    And I awoke from my dream with a smile;

It seemed like with Eternity itself I had played,

And I thought about it for a long while.


"Then suddenly, forcefully, I knew what to do:

I remembered the Dear Leader's eyes so strong;

555    I realized that I saw your eyes in them too—

That the Great Leader with me had been all along!

"Great Leader, you save us, you are us, we need you,

Like I needed the Dear Leader when danger came along;

The *Juche* Ideology has taught us to heed you,

560  Because you are Korea, and Korea is strong!"


The Great Leader smiled at what the woman had

  learned,

And once more renewed his steely resolve;

He would somehow salve what the sanctions had

  burned,

And with might and diplomacy their riddle solve.


565  Then was shown in a man most humble,

Too respectful to look the Great Kim in his eyes;

At first the man could only manage to mumble,

But the Great Leader could tell he was wise:


"It's okay, good farmer," for Kim could see

570   That the man was a worker of the soil,

"I know that my father has sent you to me,

So let no fears your conscience embroil."

# CHAPTER SEVEN: *THE VISION OF THE SCHOLAR-FARMER.*

"I was at home, reading the Dear Father's

Great words about *Socialism of our Style*;

575    For I have spent part of my life as a scholar,

And taught at Kim Il Sung University for a while.


"I left when I heard you, Great Leader, speak

Of Kimilsungism-Kimjongilism as *Juche's* light;

For I felt it was better for me to seek

580    A way to maintain *jarip*, as is right.


"You had said it all—How could I say more?

So I returned to the profession of my father:

I left behind the academic corps,

Took up the plow, and became a farmer.

585    "It was evening that day, I had finished my work,

The pages before me were warming my heart,

When suddenly something outside went berserk

And tore the fabric of the darkness apart.


"My first thought was 'It's happened, it's happened at

    last!

590    The enemy has finally released all its missiles!

Thank the Great Leader that he to *jawi* has held fast,

So that we'll maintain *jaju* from those devils.'


"The sound, it continued, like rolling thunder,

I stepped outside and looked into the skies,

595    There, like a freight-train, I saw with wonder

Thundering oxen with fire in their eyes!

"Their size was incredible—they blocked most of the

    stars;

Their bodies were as hard as corundum;

Each looked like it could pull ten-thousand freight cars,

600    With pistons for legs—a mighty conundrum!


"There were a total of twelve of these creatures;

Their hooves were like iron, their horns were like steel;

They snorted coal-steam, but their dominant features

Were those eyes that I somehow could feel.


605    "The warmth of *Juche* had now been replaced

By the fire of something I could not understand;

To our sovereign sky they'd already laid waste—

What about the *jaju* of our sovereign land?

"'Stop this treason!' I cried inside of my head,

610    'Stop thinking thoughts that divide us!

The Great Leader will show the true answer instead—

We must simply use the logic inside us!'

"I knew that you, Great Leader, maintained such *jawi*

That you had to be aware of this obvious threat;

615    As you hadn't shot them down, and their effect I could

see,

They probably shouldn't make me upset.

"If you knew of them, and their presence permitted,

They must be under your wise control;

Or else, my racing logic persisted,

620    They must be a product of my mind or my soul.

"Or perhaps, and this didn't sound right,

For I do not countenance mythology,

Maybe some entity brought this horrible sight,

And I owed many teachers an apology.


525    "For too often in class I'd argued with wisemen,

Who'd studied ancient scrolls and secret codes;

In my head I'd often despised them,

When they talked about travelling mystical roads.


"Yet on one magic creature even I could agree,

530    As for it much evidence in history abounds;

In carvings and paintings and bones I could see

The Dragons of Korea in mystery astound.

"These Dragons are thought to be sentient and wise,

Compassionate, powerful, all things commanding;

635    As a scholar and farmer had I attracted their eyes,

So that they wished to give me greater understanding?

"If so, I reasoned, maybe one of these Dragons

Had planted this powerful vision in my mind;

For I had not had a single bottle or flagon

640    Of soju, or beer, or vodka, or wine.

"But before I could reason any further

A greater sight happened even still:

The heavens parted above this observer

And climbing them was Leader Kim Jong Il!

645     "From starlight he fashioned harnesses and yokes,

From moondust he formed a gigantic plow,

He guided the oxen with vigorous strokes

From a whip he tore from the Giant's eyebrow.


"Then, led by the Chollima of Destiny,

650     The Dear Leader plowed non-arable land,

And soon everywhere great fertility

Was created by that mighty caravan.


"And then, Great Leader, I looked into his eyes,

And was overcome by their great power,

655     I collapsed and when I awoke realized,

I couldn't remain there and tremble and cower

When I had such a great story to tell:

I knew that to see you I had to come;

But I was very fearful as well,

660    Since your eyes have the power to strike me dumb:

I know the Dear Leader is your father and you

Are destined to fulfill *Juche* in the land

With your wisdom and knowledge that carry us through

What the enemies of self-reliance have planned."


665    The Great Leader smiled and said "It's okay—

I'll be gentle so you can look in my eyes.

Only one mistake have you made on your way,

But it is because you are dutiful and wise:

We need men of *Juche* like yourself to teach

670    Others their duties and reason for being.

Although I know it best it doesn't mean you can't preach

Kimilsungism-Kimjongilism in all of its meaning.

I want you to return to your university

And teach our best students what you have learned,

675    For with your understanding they will gain much

        diversity

To go with the honors and diplomas they've earned.


"But just one question I have left, my dear scholar."

"Yes, Great Leader?" the scholar-farmer said.

"Do you know if a Dragon was that evening your caller,

680    Or did someone else put that vision in your head?"


"I don't know, Great Leader---I'm not at all sure,

Though I've thought about it for a long while."

"Perhaps," said Great Kim, "if your thoughts remain

pure,

You'll discover it soon." And the Great Leader smiled.

# CHAPTER EIGHT: *THE CAVE OF JUCHE*.

585    It was late in the evening on that Holy Day,

The Great Leader was content, but knew the day wasn't

done.

Sure enough, the Adjutant came into say,

"Supreme Commander, there is yet another one."


An old man came in, built like a runner,

590    And immediately himself prostrated;

Great Kim gently helped up the newcomer

And said, "Rest easy, I have you awaited.


"It's okay, you may look at me," the Great Leader went

on,

"I will moderate my countenance—you will not be

harmed."

695    Finally on the man it began slowly to dawn

That he need not for his safety have any alarm.


He looked at Great Kim with hesitation at first,

And then finally relaxed his stiff shoulders.

"Great Leader, in the ways of the mountains I'm well-

versed,

700    For I used to be one of your mountain soldiers.


"I would patrol at the peaks keeping lookout for spies,

Run the ridges of the mountains like a wild beast;

I developed great instincts and used my hawk-eyes,

To see if enemy movements had increased.

705    "For countless kilometers I could run without ceasing,

And I learned to live independently off the land;

I never got drunk or relaxed or went feasting:

I was one of the best soldiers under your command.


"I was hiking years ago on this Holy Night,

710    At the base of the sacred peak of Paektu,

When a sudden loud roar gave me a fright,

And I tried on its sound too follow through.

But before I could move an earthquake shook

So that, like a wobbly fawn born new,

715    My legs were unsteady and I painfully took

A tumble, so all I could think of to do

Was watch out for rocks that might have been

dislodged,

And see if any enemies had been dislodged too;

When suddenly like a boulder rolled something that I

dodged,

720    And I hurried to see exactly what it was, or who.


"I soon saw it was a man and rushed to his side;

He wore the uniform of an Honor Guard;

I checked to see how he'd fared after his rough ride,

And found him okay, though shaken and scarred.


725    "He soon revived—I had given him some water,

While binding his wounds and a broken arm.

'Thank you,' he said, 'thanks a whole lot, Sir—

I thought I would come to much greater harm.'

"Then I realized who this soldier must be:

730    A member of the Special Guard for today;

For the Dear Leader's birthplace had been just above

      me,

When the earthquake forced me out of my way.


"The soldier didn't have anything to report:

The earthquake had caught him totally by surprise.

735    Our men found nothing, but I heard talk of a sort

That suggested to reflect upon this was wise.


"For along the borders in the high country,

Certain villagers told of an intriguing tale:

That on this Holy Day, very abruptly,

740    A dragon sometimes roared, and without fail;

A cavern would appear, though not all would see it,

Even though it was always on Mount Paektu;

So that most of the people did not believe it,

Except for a sincere and trustworthy few.


745    "The cave would be visible for only an instant,

And then would disappear into the rocks and the soil.

As far as anyone knew, no one had been in it,

And nobody wanted the authorities to embroil.


"After my term of service was finished,

750    I continued supporting *jaju* and *jawi*;

For my skills and abilities were barely diminished,

And my obligations I clearly could see.

"I was ranging throughout the mountains last night,

The first hour of this Day, forever consecrated,

755    On Paektu Mountain, once again near the site

Where the Dear Leader's birth had been fated.


"Suddenly I thought I heard a tiger roar;

I immediately started toward the sound;

Then, as had happened many years before,

760    An earthquake shook that Holy Ground.


"Somehow upon my feet I stayed,

Determined to find out what was taking place:

Was a great discovery about to be made,

Or was I the enemy about to face?

765   "I ran rapidly toward the sound I had heard

And looked up, and there in the mountainside,

Which I couldn't believe hadn't been observed,

Was a cave in which a large dragon could hide.


"There seemed to be a light from within,

770   And deciding this discovery was worthy of my death,

I threw caution aside and rushed recklessly in.

What I saw caused me to not just lose my breath,

But to fall on my face in reverence and awe:

For more powerful than anything I'd imagined or seen,

775   It wasn't just a red Dragon I fearfully saw,

But Kim Il Sung and Kim Jong Il, who in radiance

gleamed.

"I was faint, I did not have the strength to arise,

I had too much respect to even attempt it;

I was terrified of those three sets of eyes,

780    For they spoke of authority, and they meant it!


"'You may rise,' said a deep voice in my mind,

As the cave opening closed up behind me;

I rose to my knees wondering if I would find

Some dreadful terror with my fear to bind me.


785    "I found the light in the cave was not from a fire,

Although it did indeed come from a flame

That rose from a Torch, not kindling or a pyre:

I knew instantly 'The Torch of *Juche*' was its name.

"I gazed through the Torch into the Dragon's eyes—

790    For that is what he intended me to do;

Soon other details I began to realize,

Which his Consciousness guided me through.


"To the Dragon's right sat the Eternal President,

Kim Il Sung, on a chair cut from the cave wall;

795    The Eternal General Secretary was likewise resident

To the Dragon's left in that magnificent hall.


"The cavern of decoration was otherwise bare,

Except for the shadows cast by the Torch,

But the gigantic Dragon in his lair

800    Was enough my mind and my vision to scorch.

"But past the Torch's light his eyes calmed me down,

And I soon realized I'd been brought there to learn;

The flame of the Torch made a comforting sound

As the Ways of *Juche* I began to discern.


805    "The Eternal President was the first to speak,

Although I don't remember if I saw his lips move,

But it was Kim Il Sung's voice, and it was unique,

And his words left nothing to prove:


"'The *Juche* Ideology foremost is predicated

810    Upon *jaju*, the political independence

Of the State of Korea, which cannot be dictated

By oppressive regimes or their dependents.

"'Korea must be free her own identity to find,

Under the guidance of the Great Party Leader;

815   That is the only way Korea can be of one mind,

When opposed by the ignorant or willful unbeliever.


"'Our kind of *jaju* is unique to Korea,

And is supported by *jarip* and *jawi*;

If not, Korea would not be Korea,

820   And some other country you'd see.'


"Then spoke the Dear Leader in a similar way,

With a rational essence I could almost feel;

I listened intently to what he had to say,

Eternal General Secretary, Kim Jong Il:

825    "'Another pillar of the *Juche* Ideology

Is *jarip*, economic self-sustenance;

Not some Western economic theology,

But Korea's own style of economic maintenance.


"'It is essential we help our economy to grow

830    The Korean way, to preserve our identity.

Exactly how, the *Juche* Ideology will show,

Because with our style our socialism has empathy.


"'Korean *jarip* is supported, of course,

By Korea's own *jaju* and *jawi*;

835    Foreign sanctions attempt to knock us off course,

By destroying not just one, but all three.'

"Then spoke the Dragon, through his deep eyes—

For I suspect that his voice would have killed me.

He was compassionate, understanding, and wise,

840     And the depth of his intellect thrilled me.


"'At the Heart of *Juche* I, your Dragon, reside,

And your Dragon is the Heart of Korea;

There is not within any other mountainside,

A Being so informed by so wise an idea.


845     "'*Juche* demands a wise and perfect leader,

And, as a Dragon, I am perfection;

When you see the Great Leader you'll be a believer,

For I am his—and Korea's—perfect reflection.

"'*Jawi* remains crucial to our survival:

850    Self-reliance in defense we'll certainly protect;

We will continue our Nuclear Program's revival,

For we shall not *Juche* ever neglect.


"'You have now witnessed our pledge to the nation,

To protect *jaju*, *jarip*, and *jawi*;

855    In Kimilsungism-Kimjongilism we find our salvation,

For in no other way can Korea be free.'


"Then the Dragon put me to sleep with his eyes,

And in the morning I awoke, feeling a new power;

I looked around with new vigor and saw with surprise

860    That I was at the base of the great *Juche* Tower.

"I've had some difficulty making it to you,

For this Day is Sacred and you have many

    responsibilities;

But finally your guards let me through,

Since I had a soldier's respectability.


865    "I saw the Dragon and *Juche's* bright Flame,

But I came here to tell you what I else I discovered,

For I now know the Dragon's true Name:

The Dragon of Korea is yourself, and none other."


"The Great Kim smiled with his eyes growing deeper,

870    A loyal citizen now knew how much he cared;

"Your duty now is find other sleepers

And tell them that with you in the cave I was there.

"Everybody must come to know and believe,

That when Korea suffers, it cuts me to the Soul;

875    Kimilsungism-Kimjongilism gives us the light to achieve

The necessary strength our identity to control."


So the man went out with a new purpose in mind,

And in the mountains it would be sworn to and said,

That if you rest for a moment, a wise man you will find,

880    And give you dreams of *Juche* to sleep on in bed.

# CHAPTER NINE: *THE DREAM OF PRESIDENT TRUMP*.

President Trump sat up in bed, screaming;

The Secret Service immediately rushed in;

"It's okay," said Trump, "I must have been dreaming.

I seem to be guilty of some horrible sin."


885    Melania came in and the Secret Service went out;

She had an inkling of why her husband had screamed,

For ever since that performance he seemed to have
       doubt

About his anti-DPRK sanctions and schemes.


Which performance?  The one about which everyone
       was talking,

890    The one every nation had heard and had seen,

The one every Head of State was applauding,

From Germany's Chancellor to Great Britain's Queen.


The performance of the Symphony and Maidens so

   beautiful,

Whom the Mighty Chairman had sent to the Games;

895   Who had in perfection and art been so dutiful,

And had brought honor to their Great Leader's Name.


"If he can do this," the world's leaders thought,

"Then tell us what he cannot do;

For if his citizens as well as this have been taught,

900   Then our sanctions we can hardly renew;

For they will in discipline have enough strength

In the hardships we cause to carry them through,

And if we stretch those out for any length,

Our citizens will sympathize with his too.

905    "Look at Korea united," they also said,

"Marching and competing as one together:

So many people for this country have bled—

Why shouldn't unity such as this last forever?"

So President Trump's conscience had been stabbed,

910    And he was having great trouble sleeping,

For whenever even a short nap he grabbed,

Nightmares of Justice would come creeping.

"But Melania," he was saying, "this wasn't like before;

This dream was much, much more terrifying:

915    There was a red Dragon I hadn't seen heretofore,

Who left me in shambles and wretchedly crying.

"He let out a great roar and with fire singed my hair,

And then singed the seat of my fancy pants;

My head was on fire and my bottom was bare,

920    And all I could do was drop, roll, and dance.

"And then I realized that this Dragon I had seen,

For I looked in its eyes and I saw there great wisdom,

I saw wit and intelligence extraordinary and keen,

With the ability to discern Truth with their vision.

925    "For Melania, I tell you, those eyes were Kim's!

He is the Dragon I can with certainty say.

How can I continue to fight one like him,

Who can enter my dreams in that way?


"I know that Korea has its own identity,

930 And sanctions won't succeed and are cruel,

But I made promises and I am a political entity,

And if I yield to Kim I'll look like a fool.


"Great Kim!' he screamed as though into the sky,

"Leave me alone, I know you are right!

935 I know you can't let Korea's identity die,

But give me peace for at least one night!"


Trump curled up in a ball on his bed,

About *Juche* he was painfully learning;

For nevermore let it be written or said

940  That Trump his enlightenment wasn't earning.

# CHAPTER TEN: *THE PLATINUM MEDAL.*

The Holy Day had for the Great Leader gone well,

And the Olympics themselves were very satisfying:

Every nation in the world could now tell

That the Great Kim's diplomacy was Korea unifying.


945  Great Kim! The world has now been polled,

And normal medals don't reflect your vast sum!

Some people deserve Bronze, Silver, or Gold,

But you merit better—you deserve Platinum!


For by uniting all Korea at these Olympics

950  You have outlined for all nations a plan,

Replete with a road-map and plenty of specifics,

As to how they should lift sanctions from your land.

For it is through your brilliant diplomacy,

Exercised with confidence and lightning-speed,

955    That you have confounded United States' policy

And proven that your voice is the one all should heed.


You roar like a Dragon in the midst of a battle,

For the Dragon of Korea is who you are:

"Sanctions that defy *Juche* are useless prattle—

960    A United Korea is her own Sovereign Star!"


The people flooded the streets on that Holy Night,

Torches of *Juche* held by their strong hands;

They looked to the balcony for their Sovereign Light,

The one on which the Great Leader stands.

965    As they waited to see the Star of Korea,

A desire swept over the growing crowd,

All at once they had the same idea—

To sing praises to the Great Leader, heartfelt and proud:


"Great Leader," they sang, "we ask you to guide us,

970    You are our Deliverance, you are our heart,

With truths of Kimilsungism-Kimjongilism you will

provide us,

And let none of our enemies tear us apart!


"You are our glory! You are Korea!

You are the Dragon who overpowers our foes!

975    In your indescribable eyes your people see a

Leader no force outwits or overthrows!"

At this the Great Kim came out on the balcony,

All the people cheered with joy and with pride;

This was sincere, not some political alchemy,

980     And the voice of the people was heard far and wide:


"The Torch of *Juche* is our Sacred Light,

And the Light of *Juche* can only be you,

For you taught us for Korea's identity to fight,

And showed through Kimilsungism-Kimjongilism what to

    do!


985     "For us you have fortified the whole country!

You are Korea! You are ourselves!

When we gaze in your eyes we can never feel empty,

But always empowered and always fulfilled!"

And the Great Leader gazed out on his people,

990    And felt the warmth for them he held in his heart;

Never would he permit misunderstanding and evil

To tear his country's independent identity apart.


Through ancient past Time from Forever eternal,

The Great Leader has been destined Korea to be;

995    He is her Dear Father, kind and paternal,

Yet as powerful as a Dragon is he.


The Compassionate Dragon at the stars gazed,

And saw *Juche* in those trillion burning suns;

He thought of Kimilsungism-Kimjongilism's wise ways,

1000    And in his eyes all Korea became one.

*